Bait-Fishing For Trout

Your Guide to Rods, Reels, Lines, Baits, Tackle, Techniques, Tactics, Rigs, Reading Water, Finding Fish, and Learning the Game

Terry W. Sheely

**For my grandgirl Shaila,
who takes me fishing in the rain.**

Full-color fish illustrations on cover and pages 11, 13,
15, 17, 19, 21, 23, 24 by **Windsor Nature Discovery**.

Fish charts for sale at Windsor Nature Discovery.
www.nature-discovery.com
or call 1-800-635-4194

All inquiries should be addressed to:
Frank Amato Publications, Inc.
P.O. Box 82112 • Portland, Oregon 97282
503-653-8108 • www.amatobooks.com

Color Fish Illustrations: Windsor Nature Discovery
Other Illustrations: Brad Baker
Photography by author unless otherwise noted
Cover and Book Design: Mariah Hinds
ISBN-13: 978-1-57188-428-2
UPC: 0-81127-00262-7
Printed in Singapore

1 3 5 7 9 10 8 6 4 2

Contents

4

About the Author

Terry W. Sheely has been challenging trout for more than 40 years, from the edge of the Arctic to the deserts of the Southwest, from the Pacific to the Atlantic. He lives in Washington State along the west edge of the Cascade Mountains on a lake that he fishes year-round for wild rainbow and cutthroat trout. He is an outdoor writer/photographer, frequent contributor to fishing magazines, author of five books on outdoor recreation, co-author of eight sport-fishing books and is a columnist for boating and sport-fishing magazines. He and his wife Natalie publish the *Washington State Fishing Guide* and other regional books. Terry is a member and past president of the Northwest Outdoor Writers Association and active member of Outdoor Writers Association of America.

Introduction
The Plan—Fish On!

Whaaaahooooo...it's a rod-wrenching, reel-wrecking, line-ripping trophy of a trout.

The rod bends, line sizzles off the reel spool, there's a flash in the water and suddenly a trout—a very large trout—is cartwheeling across the surface in a silvery splatter of sun-shot spray. The lunker crashes into the water, the rod bucks, the trout leaps again and you whoop, holler and hang on.

A great way to spend a weekend, and the exciting explanation for why good trout fishermen enjoy learning the basics of bait-fishing, and unraveling the secrets that experts use to gain an edge on wary trout.

It can all seem pretty intimidating for anglers new to the game; a complicated, bewildering puzzle of rods, reels, lines, baits, bobbers, hooks, swivels, sinkers, knots, terminal rigs, casting techniques, fishing tactics, finicky fish, and several species of trout with different likes and dislikes, all mixed into a bucketful of varying water, weather, and seasonal considerations. There's even a special language and code of behavior.

Taken one step at a time, though, the puzzle of how to catch trout with bait is easy to solve, and even the mistakes can be fun on a sunny Saturday morning watching a bait ride a wisp of current into a mysteriously dark hole where maybe, just maybe, a willing trout is waiting.

This book is intended and designed to explain, diagram, and illustrate the basics of bait-fishing, one of the most productive and traditional techniques for catching trout. We'll unravel the puzzle of rods, reels, lines, and other terminal gear, teach you how to tie knots, select the ideal rigging, and attach weights and hooks.

Bait-Fishing For Trout will guide you to the right water, at the right time, using the right gear, right bait, and the right technique. Setting the hook is up to you.

A good bait-fisherman will notice subtle changes and recognize natural events that can be matched with a specific presentation that will trigger trout strikes when other methods of fishing fail.

Good bait-fishermen aren't simply bobber watchers waiting for a jerk, they're skilled anglers picking a fight with a fish that makes memories.

Let's get started.

—Terry W. Sheely

Chapter 1
Trout & Where To Catch Them

It can be confusing. Dozens of trout and char species, sub species, and regional variations swim the world's waters. But, the physical differences are often so slight that only scientists can point out the distinctions, and fishermen don't care.

To set the hook on a regular basis, trout anglers only have to recognize seven common species and understand how they feed, spawn, and move at different times of the year.

Water temperature plays an important role in where you will find trout.

When the water temperature is between 40 and 50 degrees expect to find trout just under the surface, in shallow water along the shorelines of lakes or in the riffles of streams where the slightly warmer water increases the fish's metabolism and fills the water with hatching insects, larvae, leeches, minnows, worms, frogs, crayfish—all prime trout foods.

All trout are most active, feed, and bite best where the temperature of the water is about 60 degrees, especially when that temperature is near the surface. Coincidentally, that magical 60-degree range is also the temperature at which many fish eggs and insects hatch. Trout, especially big trout, gorge on these hatches and bait-fishing can be fantastic.

In early summer, it's not unusual for water temperatures that reach into the high 70s at mid-day to drop into the 60s after the sun goes down. Summer anglers often experience the finest trout fishing of the day when the water is coolest, between sundown and dark and daylight to sunrise.

Even during the hot heat of summer, on overcast, cool, or rainy days, it's common for trout to briefly move from the cool depths into the warm shallows where food is more abundant. In the shoreline areas they feed on hatching insects like caddis, damsel-, and dragonflies, leeches, hellgrammites, and a bunch of clumsy food that falls from overhanging branches and banks. Land-based foods are called "terrestrials" and includes grasshoppers, crickets, caterpillars, bees, beetles, mice, voles, and worms. Terrestrials make excellent trout bait, and catching a peanut jar full is almost as much fun as catching a trout.

When the water is colder than 50 degrees or warmer than 70 degrees trout drop into the depths where it's cool and in most lakes and streams that's near bottom, at springs, the mouths of inlet streams, in shaded pools, or below small waterfalls.

Spring

Expect most feeding trout just beneath the surface, in the shallow shoreline edges or feeding in riffles. If the sun is bright trout will move into shade or drop into 12 to 25 feet of water. Rainbows and cutthroat in lakes may crowd into the mouths of tributary streams. Eventually they'll move upstream to spawn. In many regions the fish and game departments stock lakes with 6-to 12-inch "catchable" trout in March, April, or May. These hatchery fish, typically, will remain concentrated within a few feet of the surface for the first few weeks after being planted, and bait suspended below a bobber can be very productive. Immediately after ice-out is when lake (mackinaw) trout, which live on the bottom most of the year, will come to the surface.

Summer

Summer trout will be deep while the sun is on the water during the heat of the day, and pretty inactive. As the sun drops, trout become more active and start to feed. If insects are hatching on the surface, they'll draw trout to the top, otherwise, look for them in 20 to 30 feet of water. If you're an early riser, expect to catch trout feeding in the top 15 feet of water from daylight until the sun hits the water. As the sun climbs higher, the trout swim deeper, and will ride-out the midday hours near bottom or concentrated around cool-water springs.

Fall

As midday water temperatures cool expect trout to return to the shallows and surface feeding. Brook trout and brown trout will be moving toward and into feeder streams to spawn. Fall feeders are often binge feeders and when you find a wad of feeding trout the action can be unforgettable. You can also spend a lot of time prospecting for feeders before finding them. Streams and rivers with fall runs of spawning salmon are very good places to find rainbows, cutthroat, and Dolly Varden that follow the schools of salmon to feed on spawned salmon eggs. Single and cluster egg fishing can be terrific for trout during salmon runs.

Winter

Most trout are less active, but can be caught through the ice by bait-fishing on the bottom at depths of between 20 to 40 feet. Occasionally, in the afternoon you'll catch river trout feeding on midge flies. Roll a big juicy nightcrawler through a riffle where trout are gulping tiny midges (sometimes called snow flies) and hang-on. If you can fish open water all winter, expect to find lake trout, rainbows and cutthroat feeding in lakes from the surface to 20 feet down. Some of the largest fish of the year are caught in the dead of winter slow-trolling bait.

Rainbow Trout

The most common and widely distributed trout, rainbows (*Oncorhynchus mykiss*) thrive in lakes and streams.

What They Look Like: Olive backs, silvery sides, bright reddish stripe extending along the lateral line from the gills to the trail. Pink-red gill covers. Small black spots on the upper body and tail.

Recent hatchery plants and rainbows in large open lakes are often silver with faint stripes and spots. Spawning rainbow are very dark. Rainbows may live to 11 years. The largest on record is a 56-pound fish caught in a gill net in Jewel Lake, British Columbia in 1913. Rainbows will inter-breed with cutthroat and may show an orange throat slash. Hooked rainbows typically leap wildly and more than other trout.

What They Eat: Rainbows of less than a pound feed mostly on tiny invertebrates, zooplankton and insects/larvae. Larger rainbows, except the insect-exclusive feeding Kamloops variety in the Kamloops area of British Columbia, eat a broad variety of aquatic and terrestrial insects, minnows, crayfish, snails, salmon eggs, shrimp and leeches. 'Bows larger than 5 pounds eat small fish, and are caught on large and small baits.

Top Baits: Hellgrammites, salmon eggs in single or cluster rigs, grasshoppers, crickets, shrimp, flavored and scented marshmallows, floating-scented paste baits, minnows, leeches, small crayfish, nightcrawlers.

Where to Catch Them: Rainbows do well in lowland and mountain lakes, streams and rivers where water temperatures rarely climb higher than 65 degrees, but can tolerate temperatures in the low 80's. In the spring, and year-round in early mornings and evenings, fish near the surface and along the shore. In summer look for deep water, mouths of cooler inlets, and springs. The steelhead variety is anadromous, maturing in salt water and spawning in fresh water. Rainbows spawn from February to June preferably in flowing water. In lakes, large spawners run up tributary streams or find a gravel beach to spawn. During pre-spawn, look for concentrations of big rainbows off tributary spawning streams. Watch for rise rings or surface swirls left by feeding fish.

Cutthroat Trout

At least half-a-dozen strains and varieties of cutthroat (*Salmo clarki*) are fished for, including Lahontan, a subspecies that thrives in alkaline water so thick with potassium and salt that other fish can't live in it, and a sea-going variety that moves freely between salt and fresh water. They are the native trout of western mountain and foothill streams, and have been stocked in many high-mountain lakes.

What They Look Like: Named for the bright red orange streak in the fold under the lower jaw which is used as a defense when the trout opens its mouth to drive away other fish. Cutts are usually heavily spotted, sometimes have a golden green coloration, with bluish gray backs. Large cutts may have deep red gill covers. Nearly all cutts have lots of large black spots on the back, upper sides and tail. Small scales. The world-record cutthroat is a 41-pound Lahontan caught in Nevada's Pyramid Lake in December 1925. May reach 10 years old.

What They Eat: Small cutthroat feed mostly on aquatic flies, emergers and nymphs, but the largest fish prey almost exclusively on minnows, freshwater shrimp and other large aquatics. Small (2- to 3-inch) herring are popular baits for sea-runs. Wild cutthroat mature in three years, when they're 8 to 12 inches long.

Top Baits: Nightcrawlers are tops. Also try leeches, hellgrammites, nymphs, and grasshoppers. Salmon eggs are excellent when fishing for sea-runs behind spawning salmon or steelhead. Cutthroat almost always prefer baits with a red or yellow color. Cutts are not leapers, and when hooked usually put up a strong, twisting, bulldogging fight, occasionally wallowing to the surface.

Where to Catch Them: Cutts prefer colder water than most trout. In summer try the coldest, most shaded water available. Cutts spawn February to April and rarely later than June. They favor fast, whitewater streams but have adapted well to alpine lakes, beaver ponds and cold upland lakes. In lakes, fish for cutts in rocky areas, sandy shorelines and deep slots. In flowing water they prefer riffles or deep pools under overhanging brush and behind log jams. They do well in sea-level sloughs or at 12,000 feet in icy mountain lakes. Coastal areas of Northern California, Oregon, Washington, British Columbia and Alaska support a sea-run variety also known as bluebacks or harvest trout. In salt water, sea-runs are often caught on incoming tides over shallow gravel clam beaches, at the mouths of major tributaries, and, in the spring and fall, in rivers when they follow spawning fish upstream to prey on the eggs. Most estuaries support resident sea-runs feeding in sloughs and hiding under overhanging brush, tree branches or behind pilings.

Brown Trout

Introduced from Europe, browns (*Salmo trutta*) are sometimes regionally called Loch Levens or German browns, and are now widely distributed in rivers and lowland lakes. Browns have a deserved reputation as the wariest and most difficult trout to catch. Oddly, their closest relative is Atlantic salmon, which also have spots, but lack halos. Browns interbreed with brook trout creating tiger trout.

What They Look Like: Golden brown sides and back with large prominent black and red spots some with pale, bluish halos. The only trout with both red and black spotting. The long, lower jaw of large males often develops a wicked hook. Have been known to weigh 40 pounds, and reach 7 to 12 years.

What They Eat: Feeds on both aquatic and terrestrial insects, minnows, sculpins, crayfish, snails and occasionally frogs and mice. Feeds mostly on the bottom, but will come up for damsel, may, caddis and stonefly hatches.

Top Baits: Two- to three-inch-long bullhead sculpins are tops, followed by minnows, nightcrawlers, small softshell crayfish, hellgrammites, and clusters of salmon eggs. A grasshopper kicking on the surface at night is tough for a brown to resist. Browns seem less willing than other trout to take scented paste baits. Use the finest diameter leader you can get away with, hide the hook and use small sinkers.

Where to Catch Them: Browns don't tolerate warm (75 to 80 degree) water as well as rainbows, and will head for cool water on the bottom, or off of cold-water tributaries a lot earlier in the year. They are most active when water is in the 54- to 64-degree range. Browns are notorious night feeders and even during the heat of summer will come to the surface at night to slurp hatches of monster *Hexagenia* may-flies, mosquitoes, moths and mice. Large browns, especially, seem to favor meat over insects. In the Northeast, Europe and South America, browns, like steelhead, may be sea-going, but not on the West Coast. Browns have been heavily stocked in cold water, lowland lakes and rivers east of the Cascade Mountain Range. Very few high-mountain lakes are stocked with browns. Browns prefer pools, eddies and deep sullen runs to fast flows. If cover is available, they'll be behind it. Unlike rainbows and cutthroat, browns spawn in late fall and early winter and some of the best stream fishing is from October to February when the snow is flying. If spawning streams aren't accessible from a lake watch for spawners in the shoreline shallows on rough gravel.

Brookies

Often mistakenly called "trout," brookies (*Salvelinus fontinalis*) are actually char, closely related to Arctic char, Dolly Varden, bull trout, and mackinaw, which are also called lake trout. Char can be distinguished from trout by a thin ribbon of white on the front edges of pectoral, pelvic and anal fins. Brookies are native to the East Coast and were not brought to the West until around 1900. Now widely distributed in lakes and ponds and some streams, brookies are aggressive and fairly easy to catch. Because, unlike

trout, they spawn in still water, brookies often over-
populate small lakes and ponds, producing an over-
load of stunted 5- to 10-inch fish. In most brook trout
lakes, fish managers encourage anglers to keep a few
of these colorful fish for the skillet.

What They Look Like: Brookies are an explosion of
brilliant colors. They have stout bodies with dark
green, blue-gray or sometimes black upper bodies,
orange-red sides, white underbellies and bright
orange fins trimmed with white edging. The sides
are painted with worm-like tracks called vermiculations. They are speckled with white, red or black
spots—some encased in blue halos. The largest
brookie on record weighed only 14 1/2 pounds.
Most are 6 to 12 inches. A 3-pound brookie is a
trophy in most regions, and will have a short, thick,
deep body. Males may have kypes hooking upward
on the lower jaw. Tails are cut so straight that in
some regions brookies are nicknamed "squaretail."
Scales are exceptionally fine and so small that
some anglers mistakenly believe brookies are scale-
less. Few get older than 6 years.

What They Eat: Brookies love worms, caddisflies
and nymphs, larvae, freshwater shrimp, stoneflies,
leeches, small crayfish, and snails. They feed mostly
on or near the bottom in shaded areas with cover
but will sometimes rise to take advantage of a
heavy fly hatch.

Top Baits: The largest brookies usually fall for meat baits, especially minnows (live or preserved), and nightcrawlers. They will also take beetles, grasshoppers, hellgrammites, and occasionally a green salmon egg. Brookies seem to have a sweet tooth for green-colored baits.

Where to Catch Them: Cool water is the key to finding brookies in lakes and streams. They thrive where water temperatures are 57 to 61 degrees, rarely swim in water above 68 degrees and die if the water gets warmer than about 77 degrees. When the water's right, however, brookies thrive and can over-populate in a few years. They have been planted by fish and game departments in many lowland lakes and beaver ponds and in high-mountain lakes, many of which are now overpopulated with small fish. In their native East Coast habitat brookies thrive in big rivers, but in the West only a few rivers have fishable populations, and most brookies are caught in lakes and beaver ponds. They tend to hug the bottom, favoring dark areas, and will roam in small schools around the shoreline hunting for food. Good spots to drop a lightly-weighted nightcrawler are at the bases of beaver dams, behind sunken logs, and around large rocks. Like brown trout, brookies spawn in late fall and early winter, but unlike browns they don't need rivers. They spawn in lakes over gravel, water-logged branches and other cover from the shoreline to the deepest hole. In many brook trout lakes some of the best fishing occurs between Halloween and Thanksgiving when the lake's largest spawners are in the shallows near shore. In some regions of the world, brookies, like salmon, migrate into salt water, but not in the West.

Golden Trout

If you haven't caught a golden trout (*Salmo aquabonita*), you're in the majority. These brightly colored, finicky, usually small trout live exclusively in select high-mountain lakes and streams in the Sierras, Cascades and Rockies, and nearly always require a backpack hike to reach. This makes them all the more coveted, and catching one, of any size, is a real accomplishment that few anglers achieve. They are native to alpine lakes in the Kern River drainage of California's Sierra Mountains, and have been stocked in a few high-mountain lakes in Washington, Oregon, Idaho, Montana, Colorado and Wyoming.

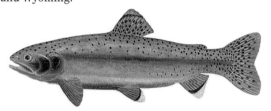

What They Look Like: Very beautiful, colorful trout, closely related to the rainbow, but much smaller. Under ideal growing conditions a mature golden will only be about 12 inches long, and in many lakes rarely grow to more than 8 inches. There are exceptions. The world record is an 11-pound fish caught in 1948 in Cooks Lake, Wyoming. In northern lakes they run smaller. Oregon's record is about 7 pounds, and Washington's largest is just under 4 pounds. Goldens are similar to rainbows, but have smaller scales, and even adults have the distinctive black parr markings along the sides. Bellies and fins are yellow to orange, gill covers are red, and a bright red band runs along the side.

The upper body is usually a yellowish green, fading to a golden-yellow below the lateral line. The major fins have white tips. One odd trait, when goldens have been brought down from high-elevation lakes in unsuccessful attempts to get them to adapt to lowland waters, they lose the gold coloration and turn blue.

What They Eat: Goldens feed mostly on small insects and microcrustacean zooplankton. They have a sweet spot for caddisfly nymphs and midges, and have been known to slurp down a grasshopper.

Top Baits: Use very small baits and lures. Top bets are natural nymphs, maggots, periwinkles, hellgrammites, and grubs, followed by bits of earthworm, single salmon eggs, and terrestrials like grasshoppers and crickets. Use small No. 10 to 16 hooks, micro sinkers and fine fluorocarbon leaders.

Where to Catch Them: The toughest part of catching goldens is finding lakes that hold them. Most fish and game departments, if asked, will reluctantly point you in the right direction, but rarely do they promote golden trout angling. In most states, these rare trout are planted only in the most remote, difficult to reach high lakes and require some seriously tough, steep hikes. In coastal mountains, goldens are nearly always above 5,000 feet elevation and in the Sierra and Rocky mountains 7,000 feet and above. They favor cold, clear water, living in lakes that are frozen most of the year and rarely get warmer than 55 degrees.

Lake Trout

Sometimes called mackinaw or gray trout, lakers (*Salvelinus namaycush*) are actually char, like brookies and Dolly Varden, that grow to enormous

proportions. One-hundred-pounders have been
recorded in Canada, which has the most lake trout
water, and the rod-and-reel record is a whopping
72-pounder. They have been stocked in many
western lakes but the further south you fish, the
smaller the fish get. The record lakers caught in
California, Washington and Oregon weighed between 30 and 40 pounds, and most weigh less than
10 pounds. They invariably live in deep, cold lakes,
often hugging the bottom in 100 feet of water most
of the year. They are predators and a very difficult
fish to catch with still-fishing techniques and most
successful bait-fishermen troll.

What They Look Like: Lakers are plain, almost col-
orless fish. Like all char they have a white ribbon
on the front edge of major fins. The bodies are gray,
lightly spotted on back and sides. The tail is deeply
forked and may be tinged with orange during early
winter spawning. They have small teeth.

What They Eat: Fish mostly, at least after they reach
2 pounds. Young lakers eat mostly crustaceans,
freshwater shrimp and insect larvae. Adults will also
eat larvae, plankton and small insects but prefer to
eat other fish—especially kokanee salmon, trout,
chubs, northern pikeminnows and whitefish.

Top Baits: Most fishermen cast, troll or jig spoons
or large plugs. Bait-fishermen, however, should
troll a large baitfish or spinner-cut strip of baitfish

just off the bottom. Herring, whitefish, kokanee and chubs are favorite baits. Check the fishing regulations. In some states it's illegal to use live baitfish or pieces of game fish. Trollers rig their baits whole, plug-cut to wobble or in long fillet strips that undulate when pulled through the water. Downriggers, wire line or several pounds of lead weight are used to get big baits deep and keep them there while trolling. Mackinaw rarely take a still-fished bait.

Where to Catch Them: Most lake trout lakes are well known, and except for a few hike-in deep water lakes in Washington's Alpine Lakes Wilderness, are accessible by highway, and trailerable boats. Look for exceptionally deep, cold, clear lakes like Odell in Oregon, Tahoe in California, Loon in Washington, Priest in Idaho, and Flathead in Montana. Lakers prefer water temperatures around 50 degrees, which for most of the year puts them on the bottom of most lakes, often more than 100 feet down. The exceptions are in the spring, usually just after ice-out, when big lakers come to the surface and inshore to feed, and in early winter when they spawn. Spring lakers sometimes hang around the shore until temperatures nudge 60 degrees, then head for the depths. They can tolerate low oxygen and extremely cold water better than most trout or char. They spawn in the fall, October to December, on ledges with rock rubble in less than 20 feet of water. November fishing can be very productive trolling baitfish along rocky shorelines.

Dolly Varden

Until a few years ago, Dolly Varden (*Salvelinus malma*) and bull trout were considered one and the same. They have since been divided into two species distinguished by habitat, and in many areas are protected by the Endangered Species Act. Dolly Varden are the sea-going cousins and are frequently found in the same areas as sea-run cutthroat trout, hanging around the mouths of major steelhead and salmon rivers, and following the bigger fish upstream to feed on their spawn. Both are char, aggressive predators, grow to more than 30 pounds, and commonly reach 5 pounds.

What They Look Like:. Like all char, Dollies have white edges on their major fins, small scales and bright colors. They are olive-green across the back and sides, white on the bellies, with orange and red spots on the sides. Sea-going fish are generally more silver. While their colors may be confused with brook trout, Dollies and bull trout both lack the worm track vermiculations found on brookies.
What They Eat: Dollies are opportunistic predators that like a good chunk of meat. Baitfish (whole, plug-cut or fillets) are tops, followed by salmon eggs (single or clusters), nightcrawlers, and shrimp.
Top Baits: Montanans used to brag about catching big Dollies on raw chicken wings, squirrel legs and hot dogs, but I'd stick with the more traditional plug-cut herring, or strip of kokanee fillet, where legal. Large minnows, chubs, and similar baitfish, trolled or drifted along the bottom, are also good.

In coastal rivers, salmon spawn and fresh herring are tops. I've had good luck shore fishing over rapidly sloping bottoms by casting and slowly retrieving preserved minnows.

Where to Catch Them: A native char, Dollies are found in fast-flowing, cold water streams and deep, cold lakes of most northern states. Bull trout in rivers prefer eddies and protected points where they can hold out of the current to ambush passing fish. Both spawn in small creeks and inlets in the early fall, and immediately after ice-out, are often schooled near creek mouths. In lakes, they follow the baitfish and will be found at the same depth as kokanee schools. Saltwater estuaries and the lower reaches of most steelhead and salmon rivers will hold Dolly Varden. These predators will follow fall salmon upstream, often holding a few yards below spawners to slurp up drifting eggs. Drifting single salmon eggs through tailouts can be incredibly productive during the salmon spawn.

Parts of a Trout

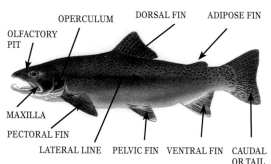

OPERCULUM DORSAL FIN ADIPOSE FIN

OLFACTORY PIT

MAXILLA

PECTORAL FIN

LATERAL LINE PELVIC FIN VENTRAL FIN CAUDAL OR TAIL FIN

Chapter 2
Bait-Fishing Tackle

Getting on the water with the right rod, reel, hook, line and sinker for the job, that's the first challenge.

Rows of rods, cases of reels, miles of monofilaments, aisles of hooks, weights, bobbers, boxes, boots...sorting through today's bewildering variety of specialized tackle can be tougher than nailing a 3-pound brown with a drifting periwinkle.

The first rule is understanding which equipment is actually needed and the second is simplicity. A good bait-fishing outfit doesn't have to be complicated, expensive or extensive, but it does have to match the bait being used and fishing conditions. And it has to be in tip-top shape!

Note to Dad, Mom and Other Instructors: If your old fishing tackle isn't good enough for you to use, throw it away. Never hand it down. It's silly to expect a beginner to learn with gear that frustrates and defeats seasoned fishing veterans.

Fishing for trout is tough enough, don't make it harder by handicapping newcomers with bad gear. Learning to fish should be fun and it never is when the rod has worn guides, the reel handle wobbles, spools stick, line kinks, hooks are rusted, and bobbers sink. Only an expert bait-fisherman with years on the water has the experience to overcome worn, abused or inappropriate tackle. Beginners can't be expected to learn how to fish AND conquer frustrating tackle snarls. Take it a step further: Those without any experience handling tackle need better equipment than veteran anglers.

Rods

They come in dozens of styles, hundreds of shapes, thousands of sizes and specifications, but basic bait-fishing rods for trout can be boiled down to two easily-mastered styles: spinning, where an open-face, bail-arm reel is mounted under the rod; and spin-cast, where a closed-face, push-button reel is mounted on top of the rod. Try both before choosing. Many instructors believe spin-casts are easier for beginners to learn, but most novice anglers, I've found, easily master spinning rods. Pay no attention to the "bait-casting" rod favored by steelhead and salmon anglers. While these handsome outfits are made for bait-fishing, they are specialized fishing tools and are a lot tougher for beginners to master. Only very expensive, high-end models have the delicate actions that good trout bait-fishermen need to cast and control thin-diameter lines, ultralight sinkers and nearly weightless baits.

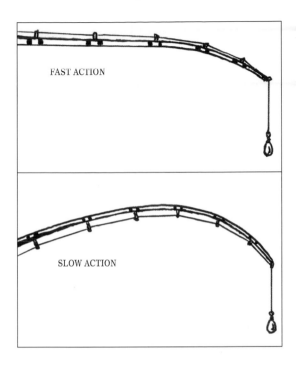

Spinning and spin-cast rods that will be used for bait-fishing should have several unique requirements that actually combine two completely opposite rod actions. A stiff rod has what's called a "fast" action. Flexible rods, on the other hand, are referred to as "slow." A good bait-fishing rod will be a combination of both fast and slow actions.

The tip section should be "fast," sensitive enough to signal light bites, and produce quick, solid hook-sets.

The backbone of the rod, however, should be "slow" flexing from the handle to where the tip starts. This long soft bend develops rod speed gradually, and allows delicate baits like ghost shrimp, fresh salmon eggs and live insects to be gently lobbed a long way. Stiffer, "fast" rods develop crack-the-whip casting velocities that may rip sharp hooks through delicate baits during the cast.

Look for rod ratings and specifics to be imprinted just above the handle.

When matching reels and rods, remember that the first line guide on a spinning rod is an oversize "gathering ring" that squeezes down the loops unwinding from the spool of the reel. Spin-casting rods won't have gathering rings. In a pinch, you can use a spin-cast reel on a spinning rod, but never use a spinning reel on a spin-cast rod because the unfolding line loops will jam in the small first guide.

When casting and fishing the guides are aligned on top of spin-cast rods, and on the underside of spinning rods.

Look for These Trout Rod Features: Two-piece spin or spin-cast model (one-piece rods are actually more sensitive but can be expensive and awkward to pack), from 5 1/2 to 6 1/2 feet long, rated as a "medium" or "medium-light" action, and built to cast 1/16 to 1/2 ounces, with 2- to 6 pound-test line. For bait-fishing, I'll choose flexible, slow fiberglass or fiberglass-graphite composite rods over "fast" rods built of graphite or Boron. Fast rods are excellent for rocket-casting artificial lures, but a bit too stiff for delicate bait presentations.

Reels

Buy the Reel That Fits Your Rod: Top-mounted-push button spin-cast reels go on spin-casting rods with small line guides.

Under-rod mounted open-face spinning reels must go on spinning rods with a large gathering ring for the first guide. It's important that reels balance in size and weight with your rod. Reels that weigh 5 to 7 1/2 ounces balance with most 6-foot trout rods.

The spool will hold at least 120 yards of 6-pound-test line, and the reel will have a gear retrieve ratio of between 4:1 and 6:1. The higher the ratio number, the faster that line can be retrieved, which is important when playing lightning-quick trout.

Pick a reel that has a velvet-smooth drag system. When you finally tie into that "big one" you don't want a ragged drag to seize and pop the line.

To test the drag on a reel that isn't spooled with line, lock the empty spool in place with the anti-reverse lever, then use your fingers to rotate it clock-wise, gradually increasing tension. A dependable drag will slide with a silkiness that doesn't catch or jerk. Also check the location of the tension adjustment. You want it positioned where it's easy to reach on that big-trout day when you need to increase or decrease line tension in a hurry.

Whenever possible test the drag with line on the reel. Try this. With the anti-reverse lever locked, have your buddy grab the line and walk away, taking line (just like a whopper of a trout running for deep water) while you hold the reel and adjust drag tension. If the drag slips smoothly and evenly—no jerks—buy it.

Set the drag to slip at about half the breaking strength of your line. If your line is factory rated to break at 6 pounds, set the drag to slip at 3 pounds of pull.

The handles on most modern spinning reels, even inexpensive models, can be swapped from

Dave Killhefner

side-to-side for either left- or right-hand retrieves.
Spin-cast reels, however, are almost always available only with the handle mounted on the right
side for right-hand retrieves. Some manufacturers
offer a limited range of left-hand spin-cast reels,
but it's easier and less costly for left-handers to
just switch hands after casting.

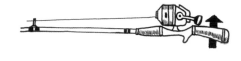

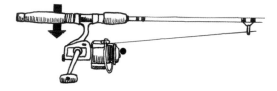

A common mistake is mounting reels in the
wrong place.

Push-button, closed-face reels are designed to be
mounted on top of the rod. There are a few closed-
face reels that mount under rods but instead of hav-
ing push-button releases they are built with triggers.

Mount your open-face spinning reel under the
rod, hanging down, so that when the bail is open
for casting the line can be pressed against the rod
handle with a fingertip. On the forward cast lift the
finger and the line flies.

Lines

Lines have come a long way in recent years and
with those improvements came the usual confusion.

Monofilament, fluorocarbon, braided, Dacron,
fiber filament, nylon, gel-spun, polyethylene fiber,

poly bonded, resin, silicone coated, high visibility, low visibility and no visibility...what do you pick? Monofilament is tough, thin and inexpensive; fluorocarbon is invisible and thin; braids are thin and strong; high viz is easy to see and control; low viz is tough to see; and no viz—well, it just disappears under water.

When making the selection, consider that you'll be using spinning and spin-cast reels with large spools, adding sinkers, tying into swivels and dragging bait along the bottom, around snags and in weed beds.

With spinning and spin-cast reels I like a quality limp (stiff lines tend to tangle when the loops are pulled off spinning reel spools), low-stretch monofilament, with a small diameter, coated for abrasion resistance and casting ease. A breaking strength of 4 pounds covers most bait-fishing situations, but if a lot of large fish are around, it doesn't hurt to step up to 6-pound. To this mainline, connect several feet of high-quality leader of ultra-thin diameter fluorocarbon line from 1- to 6-pound test. The fine diameter and invisibility of the fluorocarbon leader allows a natural looking bait presentation, doesn't spook leader-shy lunkers, and in snaggy cover I can switch to a heavier breaking strength and still be invisible to line-shy fish.

Making the Cast
Spin-Casting

1. Grasp the pistol grip behind the reel. Put your other hand in front of the reel and pinch the line lightly between the thumb and forefinger. Hold the line, depress the release button with the thumb of the back hand and hold it down.

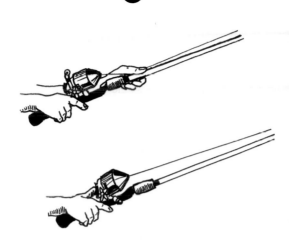

2. Face target area, and turn slightly so the arm holding the rod handle is slightly closer to the target. Hold rod tip level with your eyes, "aiming" at target area.

3. With just your forearm, snap the rod swiftly, smoothly straight up and stop. The rod will bend backward.

4. Snap the rod forward and when it passes eye level release the push button and your grip on the line. If the lure lands short you released the thumb button too late. If the lure overshoots or goes straight up you released the button too soon. With a little practice you'll get the feel of it.

Spinning

1. Grip the rod handle with your master hand, positioning the reel stem between the second and third fingers. Place the thumb on top of the handle. With your forefinger touch the spool and pick up the line and press it against the underside of the rod handle in front of the reel. Hold the line tight, and with the freehand cock or open the line bail.

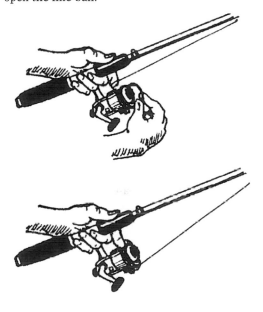

2. Continue to hold the line against the rod and face the target. Turn your body so that your eye, shoulder, rod arm and rod tip—at eye level—are pointed at the target.

3. In one swift, smooth movement, bend your casting arm at the elbow raising your arm and rod until your hand is at eye level. Stop.

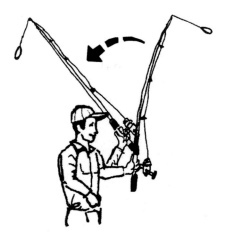

4. The rod will continue to bend backward, loading. With no hesitation, snap it forward with a slight wrist movement. When the rod drops to about eye level, release the line. As the bait nears the target area "feather" it into the strike zone by lightly touching the line.

5. If it's going to sail past, touch the spool and stop the line to drop it on target. Practice.

The Point of Hooks

The size and type of bait you're using will determine the style and size of the hook. These illustrations match basic hook styles and sizes with recommended baits. The larger the number the smaller the hook size. For example the tines on a No. 6 are larger than on a No. 12. Buy a hook sharpener and use it often. All hooks, except laser- and acid-honed styles, need sharpening right out of the box. Hook color is mostly a matter of personal preference. I prefer bronze-colored hooks when using live bait, cluster eggs or paste baits, and gold hooks with single salmon eggs. Red hooks seem to increase the effectiveness of cluster eggs, herring and shrimp.

Single Salmon Eggs

Hooks used with single salmon eggs are in sizes ranging from No. 6 to No. 14. These tiny hooks also work well with periwinkles, maggots, hellgrammites and small grubs.
Recommended: No. 12

Worms, Marshmallows

Baitholder-style hooks have a pair of keeper barbs on the outside of the shank below the eye, and in No. 10 to No. 6 are excellent hooks to match with worms, marshmallows, grasshoppers, crickets, shrimp and other small live baits.
Recommended: No. 8

Minnows, Nightcrawlers

Long-shank hooks are designed for bulky baits such as minnows (live or preserved), crayfish, frogs, leeches and large nightcrawlers. No. 6 to No. 10 will handle most situations.
Recommended: No. 8

Paste Baits

The two additional tines on treble hooks provide the gripping surface needed to keep soft baits such as cheese, flavored marshmallows, and scented

paste baits, like Power Bait, attached securely. The baits should be molded around the shank inside the tines with a thin veneer draped over the tines. For trout, use small trebles No. 8 to No. 14. These are good hooks when you're fishing for lunch, but if you intend to release fish, don't use this style. Trebles commonly injure fish too severely to survive.
Recommended: No. 12

Cluster Eggs

Clusters of salmon eggs, shrimp and herring (plug cut or filleted into spinners) are popular baits for anadromous trout such as sea-run cutthroat, Dolly Varden and steelhead. Use larger, stainless or bronzed

hooks No. 4 to 2/0; No. 1 or 1/0 are good all-around sizes. I've also had success by rigging these bulky baits on double-tined hooks.
Recommended: No. 1

Sand Shrimp

Specialty hooks designed for long soft baits like sandshrimp have double tines, and extraordinarily long shanks. A safety pin is braided to the shank for securing the bait. These hooks are not common, but do a good job of pinning long soft baits to the shank.
Recommended: No. 6

Getting Down With Sinkers

Trout can be fussy biters, especially when they have time to leisurely inspect a bait, which for bait-fishermen is most of the time. And that's why sinker selection is every bit as important as deciding which hook to use and which bait will work best.

There are at least a dozen sinker styles in most tackle departments and each has a specific use. Trout fishermen, though, can cover most bait-fishing situations with just three styles: split shot, sliding egg, and rubber-core clincher.

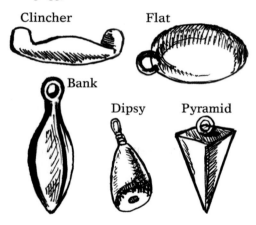

Clincher Flat

Bank

Dipsy Pyramid

Tip: Heavy weights spook fish, rough up lines, and snag bottom. Always use the lightest sinker you can get away with.

Split Shot

The most versatile and common style used by bait-fishermen. Available in sizes from pinhead-size micro shot to marble-like No. 1 cannonballs.

Uses: Casting, bobber fishing.

When fishing with bait suspended below a bobber or when casting and retrieving, and drifting with the current along the bottom. Squeeze, gently, onto the line at least 18 inches above the bait. When using light leaders squeeze shot onto the mainline above the delicate leader. When you need more than one shot use all the same size shot and position them in a short row, touching each other to decrease tangles.

Recommended: Reusable squeeze-on/off style, in a variety dispenser pack ranging in size from BB to No. 1. My favorite, No. 7 size shot

Sliding Egg

Fishing line runs completely through this egg-shaped sinker and can slide freely so there's no "weight" feel to spook a trout mouthing the bait.

Uses: Stillfishing.

An excellent choice for all still fishing situations, including salmon eggs and worms, and floating baits like marshmallows, paste baits, cheese and combination baits. Works very well in weedy or mossy areas where the bait needs to float up from the bottom. In a pinch, sliding egg sinkers can be used for trolling bait if a stopper (swivel or split shot) is positioned to stop it from sliding down the line into the hook.

Recommended: Variety pack from 1/4 to 1 ounces My favorite, 3/8 ounce

Rubber-Core Clinch

Available in weights from 1/8 ounce to 1 1/2 ounce

and longer than they are wide, with a horizontal slot for the line to lay in. This stream-lined weight comes with and without the rubber core which protects the line from nicks. Keel sinkers are similar in shape, size and use and have built-in bead-chain swivels that do a good job of preventing line twist.

Uses: Trolling, casting to deep water.

Position on mainline at least 3 feet ahead of bait when trolling in the top 20 feet of water. The further the weight is away from the bait, the more action the bait will have. When trolling deeper than 20 feet, without a downrigger or wire line, use large crescent-shaped sinkers, like those commonly used for salmon fishing, in weights from 1 to 8 ounces. By adding a stopper knot or split shot to stop line creep, large clinch sinkers can be used while casting when you want to crawl a bait along the bottom in deep water.

Recommended: Variety packs that include a selection of rubber-cores from 1/4 ounce to 1 ounce. My favorite is 1/2 ounce

Swivels

Trout fishermen need swivels for two reasons:
1) connecting lines, sinkers and bait rigs, and 2) preventing line tangles and twist. Swivels typically come in three colors: black, brass and green. The bright color of brass sometimes attracts trout in colored water and, unfortunately, trout sometimes pass up the bait to strike the bright, but hookless swivel.

Three types of swivels will handle almost all bait-fishing situations.

Snap

The most common
type of swivel, but
one of the least

important for bait-fishermen. Its primary function
is to connect lines with lures and to rotate freely
which prevents line twist. Ball-bearing snap swivels
are superior to friction models in preventing line
twist. Bait hooks should not be directly connected
to snap swivels. The bulk detracts from the natural-
ness of the bait and impedes movement.

Uses: A connection between the mainline and
snelled hook leaders.

Recommended: Black, size 10 to 14

Barrel

One of the most useful swivels for bait-
fishermen. Line connection loops on
both ends. Available in sizes from tiny
20s to big 5/0. Most trout fishing situations require size 14-10. Barrel swivels
are simply connectors that rotate in the
center to prevent line twists.

Uses: Attach mainline to leader, as stop-
pers that prevent sliding sinkers from riding down
onto hooks, and to prevent line twists while trolling
or casting bait.

Recommended: Black, size 12

Three-Way

Line-connection loops on three sides, some models
have a swivel in the center.

Uses: A connector rigging mainline, leader and a
dropper line that leads to a sinker. Used by river or
creek fishermen who attach a string of split shot to

a few inches of dropper line that bounces along the bottom between the mainline and several feet of baited leader.

Recommended: Black, size 8

Bobbing With Bobbers

Trout feed mostly on insects, and most insects develop as pupae and nymphs and hatch into flies within 10 feet of the surface, which means that feeding trout are often found within a few feet of the surface. This makes trout ideal targets for fishermen suspending baits below bobbers. Hatchery-stocked trout, in fact, spend almost all of their first several weeks in a lake swimming in the top 10 feet of water. Spring and fall spawners swarm the shorelines and shallow inlets, and even in the heat of summer trout slip out of the cool depths from dusk till dawn to feed on nymphs, mosquitoes, fly hatches, grasshoppers, beetles, bees, crayfish, leeches, and even small mice. Fly-fishermen use foam bobbers called strike indicators to suspend artificial nymphs and wet flies. The system works just as well with real nymphs and bait.

Bobbers have three functions: provide casting weight making sinkers unnecessary, holding bait at a specific depth (say, just above the top of a weed bed) and revealing, or indicating, bites.

There are two types of floats to consider: round and quill (or pencil shaped).

Round ones are generally inexpensive, plastic and highly visible. The ball shape is difficult to pull under, except for the very small ones, which are more sensitive, but difficult to see and frequently sink under the weight of a baited hook.

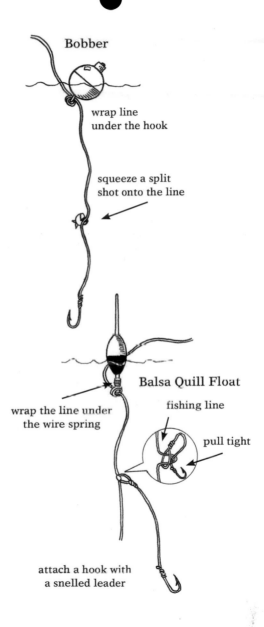

Bobber

wrap line
under the hook

squeeze a split
shot onto the line

Balsa Quill Float

wrap the line under
the wire spring

fishing line

pull tight

attach a hook with
a snelled leader

Quill or pencil shape floats made of balsa wood or plastic are superior to round models. The streamline shape is sensitive to light bites, offers no resistance when pulled under, floats high above the surface for easy visibility, and the spring-loaded line catch rarely slips but can be quickly adjusted to change depths.

Recommended: Balsa quill floats, orange or other bright colors.

Dave Kilhefner

Chapter 3
Hot Baits: How To Hook 'Em,
When To Use 'Em

Single Salmon Eggs

Use: Still-fished on bottom, still-fished below bobber, drifted downstream.

When: Year-round in lakes; best spring and fall in moving water.

Hook: No. 10-14 egg hook.

How: Insert hook point inside bottom of egg, slide up shank, rotate egg above hook point, re-seat on point.

Rating: Excellent year-round, especially productive for recent hatchery plants and when native fish are spawning.

Floating Paste/Mallow Baits

Use: Whenever fishing weedy or mossy bottoms. Still-fished on bottom, very good for suspending buoyant, scented mallows with worms or floating paste baits (Power Bait) above moss or weeds.

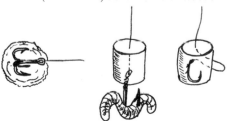

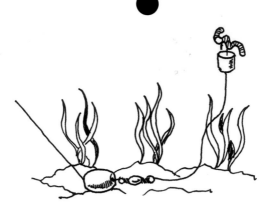

When: Year-round in lakes and ponds.
Hook: With marshmallow and worm use No. 10-8 baitholder. With Power Bait and other floating paste baits use No. 12-14 treble.
How: Marshmallows: Insert hook point in one side of mallow and out the other side, pull out a few inches of leader and make another insertion so the line loops through and around marshmallow. Pull out hook point and impale a worm at the collar so that both ends are free to wiggle.
Paste Baits: Mold onto the treble hook so that floating bait completely encases the hook points and eye.
Rating: Best in spring, and mid-summer when weed and moss growth swallow baits fished on the bottom. These floating baits suspend above bottom, above weed and moss, and in the sight range of cruising trout. The highly visible, powerfully scented paste baits will draw trout in winter either fished through the ice or bank fished.

Nightcrawlers

Use: Still-fished on bottom or under bobber; cast and retrieve near bottom and weedbeds;

downstream drifted in flowing water either free or with split shot; trolled alone or to sweeten lures.

When: Year-round. One of the best winter baits.

Hook: Baitholder style, size No. 10 to 6. Match size of 'crawlers.

How: Insert hook point under "collar" once so it can wiggle. Do not bunch on hook.

Rating: Always a top choice. Extremely versatile year-round, especially in cold water, slow bite conditions and when water is high and off-color. A super choice in small streams when drifted without sinkers into pools, beside logs and under overhanging branches.

Cluster Salmon Eggs

Use: Most often used in coastal rivers where resident trout, jack steelhead, sea-run cutthroat and Dolly Varden char are feeding on the spawn of salmon and steelhead. Also productive in large lakes, still-fished on the bottom in the flow from tributary inlets.

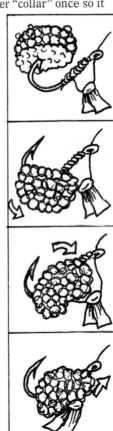

When: Best spring, fall and winter.
Hook: Short-shank, wide gap in No. 4 to No. 1.
How: Drifted on the bottom of flowing water in lakes and rivers.
Rating: Very good in rivers, and rarely used in lakes. Cluster eggs are a favorite of lake fishermen targeting only large trout.

Terrestrials & Periwinkles

Use: Drifted with split shot in small creeks, rivers. In ponds and protected stillwater bays on surface or just off bottom.

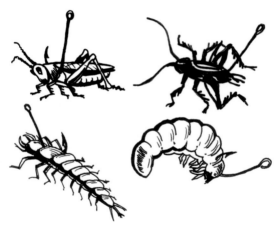

When: Summer, fall. Grubs are good for winter ice-fishing.
Hook: Small, bait-holder styles sized to match the size of the bait. Try No. 12's.
How: Still-fished or drifted with micro-split shot. Crickets and grasshoppers have natural buoyancy and will float off bottom like a paste bait or marshmallow. Grubs, periwinkles (caddis larvae shucked from the case), and hellgrammites are common

food sources in streams and rivers, and productive baits drifted with just enough sinker weight to bounce lightly along bottom. Hook once behind head, and position 12 to 20 inches below weights.
Rating: These are natural food sources for trout in most waters and are very productive, especially in late afternoon and evening. The secret is to select hook and sinker sizes that do not overpower or compromise a natural presentation. The natural buoyancy and food value of crickets and hoppers makes them perfect for still-fishing with sliding sinkers on the bottom in deep water during the hot part of the day.

Minnows

Use: Lakes and large river pools, still-fished, trolled or cast and retrieved. Especially good for the chars.

When: Late spring, summer, early fall for large trout and char. Late fall/winter for spawning browns. Winter ice fishing.
Hook: Long-shank, straight or upturned eye, Kirby or Aberdeen style No. 8 to No. 6.
How: Live minnows including sculpins (bullheads)

should be hooked just under the dorsal fin and above the spine. Do not break the spine. Dead or preserved minnows work best hooked through both lips, bottom to top and trolled or retrieved to impart action. Use as little sinker weight as possible and position weights at least 18 inches from bait.
Rating: In some states it is illegal to fish with live minnows. Check your local regulations carefully. Live and preserved minnows are very efficient trout-getters, and are a favorite bait for anglers targeting larger predator rainbows and browns and especially chars which prey on other fish. I have good luck catching beaver-pond brook trout on lip-hooked preserved minnows. The smaller the minnow the better for brookies. Large brown trout are often suckers for live bullhead sculpin. A meat-baited minnow trap will provide plenty of fishing bait in most lakes, where legal.

Leeches and Eels

Use: Mostly in lakes and stillwaters, especially with tule and weed beds.

When: Late spring, summer.
Hook: Long-shank, straight or up-eye, Beak Point or Aberdeen style No. 10 to No. 6.
How: Hook once in the head or lips, inserting hook point through the top of the head and out the bottom. Hooked top to bottom the leech will swim right side up. Add sinker weight 20 inches above the bait. Cast and retrieve, slowly. May be drifted

along the bottom from a wind-drifted boat. Try
all depths. Especially productive just above weed
beds, at inlets, and springs, and along the bottom
of drop-offs.

Rating: Leeches, more than eels, are an important
food for larger trout, especially rainbows and Kamloops, and usually provoke explosive strikes. Select
leeches that are 2 to 4 inches long.

Crayfish

Use: Lakes, rivers and rocky streams.
When: Late spring, summer.

Hook: Long-shank, straight-eye, Carlisle or Aberdeen style No. 6.

How: Insert the hook point into the underside of
the tail and out the top through the second or third
hinge. Fish without weights or lightly weighted,
with small split shot positioned 12 inches ahead of
hook. Cast and retrieve just fast enough to prevent
the bottom crawler from ducking under a rock.
Also can be drifted on lake bottoms from slow-
moving boats.

Rating: Few small trout will tackle a live crayfish,
but large, trophy-size fish find them hard to pass
up. Use very small crayfish, ideally softshells under
2 inches. Some anglers de-claw their baits.

Shrimp

Use: Drifting rivers or small streams, some potential for still-fishing lakes.

When: Year-round in rivers and streams, summer in still water.

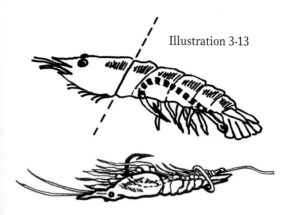

Illustration 3-13

Hook: Match hook to the size of the shrimp. Long-shank hooks, Carlisle or Aberdeen style. Also try offset hooks used by bass fishermen for rigging plastic worms. Sizes No. 6 to No. 1/0. Mustad offers a long-shank shrimp hook with a safety-pin clasp.

How: Shrimp are fished either whole or as tails (Illustration 3-13). Because they are saltwater creatures, shrimp are fished as dead bait in fresh water, attracting predatory trout with a strong, edible scent. Give trout time to home in on the scent trail.

Hook points are inserted through the top of the first hinge in the tail, pulled through the bottom and reinserted in the body. Bury the hook eye in the end of the tail. Some shrimp, especially popular ghost or sand shrimp, are delicate and will need to be secured to the shank with knotless string or tiny rubber bands. Mustad (see hooks) manufactures a long-shank bait hook with a built-in safety-pin and clasp that holds shrimp. I prefer knotless string. If fishing tails, decapitate the head behind the shell just in front of the uppermost tail hinge.

Rating: Popular and productive bait in coastal rivers for steelhead trout, sea-run cutthroat and Dolly Varden char. Small, popcorn shrimp work best in lakes with large trout. Even the grocery store variety of small peeled shrimp tails have an appeal to large trout. Should be fished slowly just off bottom, usually in deeper water.

Spinner Cuts

Use: Trolled or cast and retrieved. Saltwater shorelines, coastal river estuaries, large rivers and reservoirs with baitfish that are 3 to 5 inches long.
When: Year-round, very good for mackinaw when fished shallow in rocky ledge areas just after ice-out

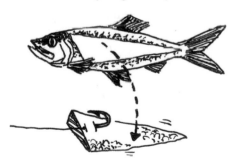

Hook: Long-shank Siwash, Aberdeen with straight eye. No. 6 to No. 1. Turned-eyes exert a side pressure that will unbalance bait.
How: Cut a long triangulated section from the side of a baitfish such as herring, anchovy, chub, native

minnow, or northern pikeminnow. Make sure the edges of the triangle are sharp and clean. Insert hook point into the wide end of the spinner at the top. Pull point through scale side but bury the shank inside the meat. The triangulated side will roll and flash when trolled or cast and retrieved. Must be fished with a barrel swivel tied-in 15 to 25 inches above the bait to eliminate line twist.

Rating: This is a bait to use when targeting predatory fish like mackinaw, sea-run cutthroat or Dolly Varden. It is especially good cast or trolled over shallow gravel saltwater beaches and in estuaries for sea-runs and Dollies. A good bait to try in large lakes inhabited by big, meat-eating trout. One of the few baits that will provoke Mackinaw to bite in the heat of the summer when they're holding in very deep water.

Chapter 4
Knots: Keep 'Em Simple and Easy-to-Learn. Loosen up those fingers, find the line cutters, it's knot-tying time.

Learning to tie fishing knots doesn't have to be intimidating. It just seems that way. Actually, just a handful of basic knots that can be learned in a few evenings at the kitchen table will handle every situation a bait-fisherman will encounter.

It is critical, however, to practice until you consistently tie solid knots that don't slip. All knots slip just before breaking. No slip, no breaks. Whenever you lose a bait rig to a snag (don't even think about breaking off a trophy trout), check the end of the line. If the monofilament is slightly curled at the break, it was knot failure.

If there is one mistake I can talk you out of making, it would be DON'T TRY TO TIE KNOTS WITH SHORT LINES!

If there's a hundred yards of line on the reel, you can spare 10 inches to make knot-tying a breeze. If you want a good giggle, watch a fisherman bite his tongue, chew his cheek and twist his fingers for two minutes trying to tie a knot with a half-inch of leader. Use a lot of leader and snip off anything that's left right at the knot. Knot stubs collect moss and weeds, tear bait, alarm fish and if your knot doesn't slip, they're not needed.

Here are a few dependable easy-to-learn, easy-to-tie knots worth learning.

Arbor

Use: Attach mainline to reel spool.

1. Pass line over and around spool arbor.
2. Tie a single overhand knot around the mainline.
3. Tie a second overhand knot in the tag (short) end of the line.
4. Pull mainline and snug arbor knot against spool.

Clinch

(Sometimes called Cinch or Fisherman's Knot)
Use: Connect mainline to hook eye, snap swivel or barrel swivel.

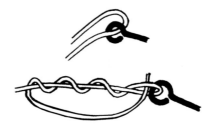

1. Pass 6 inches of mainline through eye of the hook.
2. Make 6 turns around mainline.
3. Thread tag end through line loop between hook eye and first twist.
4. Pass tag end through the large loop, hold it taut, and pull on the mainline to tighten coils. Clip tag end.

Palomar

Use: Connect mainline to hook eye, snap swivel or barrel swivel.

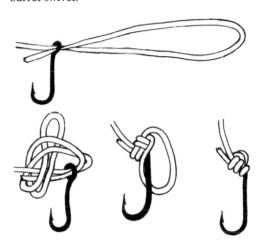

1. Pass 4 inches of mainline through hook eye, front to back, then double it back and pass it through the eye back to front.
2. Tie a loose overhand knot in doubled line in front of hook eye.
3. Pull the doubled line through the knot into a loose loop, and pass the hook through the loop.
4. Pull tag end and mainline to tighten. Clip excess tag close to knot.

Uni Basic

Use: This knot is so versatile that minor variations of it can be used to connect to hooks and swivels, join two lines, snell hook shanks and create dropper loops. Once you master the basic illustrated knot, you'll discover many ways to adapt the universal knot to specific needs.

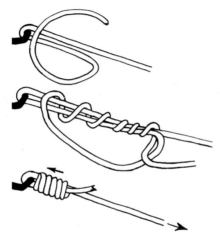

1. Thread 6 inches of mainline or leader through hook eye and double it back so that tag end and mainline lie parallel. Hold the two lines two inches above hook eye and pull the tag end back to the eye.
2. Run tag end through loop and make six wraps around both parallel lines, working from the hook up the line.
3. Hold the lines together and pull smoothly on the tag end, compress and snug the knot against the mainline.
4. Hold the knot and pull on main line and slide knot down to seat against hook eye.

Uni Line Link

Use: Join two lines, splice in additional mainline or connect leader to mainline without a barrel swivel.

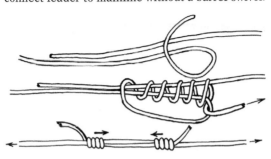

1. Lay the tag ends of both lines parallel in opposite directions, with about 6 inches of overlap.
2. With the right tag end make the basic 6-wrap knot (see Uni Basic illustration). Pull tight.
3. With the left tag end, tie another basic 6-wrap knot. Pull tight.
4. Moisten the few inches between the two knots, grasp both lines and pull in opposite directions, sliding the two knots together. Trim both tag ends as close to the knot as possible.

Snell

Use: Attach leaders directly to hook shank. By pushing the mainline front to back through the eye, a loop is formed along the shank that can be used to secure sand shrimp, cluster eggs and other soft baits firmly to the hook shank.

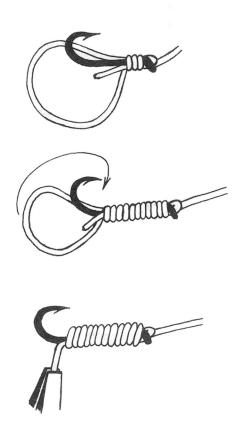

1. Run mainline through eye front to back. Double back to form a large loop below eye.
2. Hold main and tag lines against shank, and with tag end wrap both lines to the shank. Six wraps.
3. Adjust fingers to hold coils in place against shank and pull the mainline, drawing loop under coils. Use pliers to cinch down knot. Clip excess tag line.

Dropper Loop

Use: Create a loop in the mainline for connecting dropper lines. Often used for tying in dropper lines for sinker weights or attaching snelled hook above sinker.

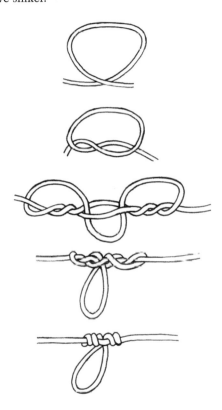

1. Form loop in line.
2. Turn loop around the standing line, keeping the center of the loop open.
3. After 8 turns, reach through the center of the loop and pull remaining line through loop.

4. Hold loop with teeth and pull both ends in opposite direction, seating wraps.
5. Pull tight until loop stands erect, perpendicular to line.

Surgeon's End Loop

Use: Form a loop in the end of mainline for attaching snelled leaders.

1. Double the line and tie a loose overhand knot.
2. Bring the doubled line through the loop a second time.
3. Hold the main and tag lines. Pull on loop and tighten knot against mainline. Clip tag excess.

Chapter 5
Riggings: Productive Bobber, Casting, Trolling, and Still-Fishing Techniques

Bobbers & Floats

Floats are especially productive early in the season when trout are feeding just under the surface and in the shallows. Floats may be rigged stationary on the line or as a slider which is preferable when fish are more than a few feet deep.

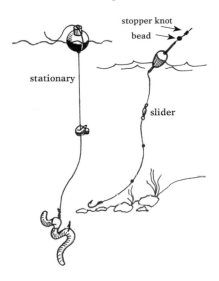

To rig a slider, clip the mainline at the pre-ferred fishing depth (for example: 12-foot bottom, 10 feet of line). Slide the bobber onto the leader section, then add a small bead stopper, and retie the line using a universal knot. The small knot that joins the leader and mainline will pass through the rod guides when cast, but will stop the bead and bobber from riding up the line past the pre-set depth. To the leader section, add a barrel swivel, enough split shot weight to pull the line through the float and a baited hook. You'll be able to reel up to the barrel swivel for casting, and then return to the pre-set depth while fishing.

Casting

Casting is a very effective way to locate schools of fish or to quickly prospect a new fishing area. The secret of casting is to use a slow-action rod and a soft lob cast that enters the water gently and doesn't rip the soft bait loose from the hook.

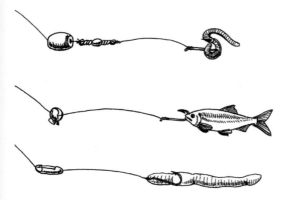

Because of the impact of casting and fish that generally swoop quickly to nail moving baits, lines need to be a little stouter than when still-fishing. A typical casting rig would be 6- or 8-pound test mainline and 4- to 6-pound leader.

The three rigs illustrated are productive in still water or slow-flow streams. Always retrieve slowly, pausing frequently to let the bait sink and to provoke strikes from trailing trout. It's always better to tie a barrel swivel at least a foot in front of the bait and behind the sinker weight to prevent line twist, and prevent the sinker from riding down to the hook.

Still-Fishing

A very popular and productive technique for fishing from piers, shorelines, and anchored boats. Boats sometimes wind-drift still-fishing rigs to locate feeding fish.

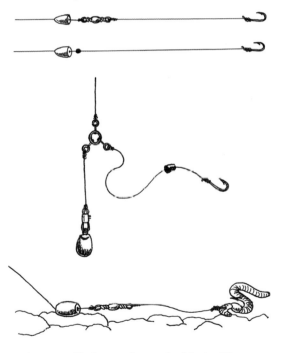

A score of baits can be used with the illustrated rigs, including single salmon eggs, cluster eggs and paste baits molded onto treble hooks. Scented floating paste baits may be rigged as the three-way swivel rig shown and the egg sinker rig as shown.

Because trout usually lightly slurp in still-fished baits (with no strike impact) and casting is minimal, still-fishermen may use finer lines than most other bait rigs. A typical trout rig would be 6-pound-test mainline and 2- to 4-pound-test leader.

The arch enemy of all still-fishermen is slack line. It's impossible to detect subtle trout bites with slack in the line because slack absorbs the energy of the bite that should vibrate your rod tip.

Try this. Softly lob a cast, allow the rig to settle to the bottom, place the rod in a holder and then reel in line until it's tight. If the weight pulls free and slides along the bottom creating slack, add weight until it holds. When still-fishing from a boat, use two anchors, one in the front and one in the back, to stabilize the craft enough to prevent sinkers from dragging.

Trolling

Trolling is the quickest way to locate trout holding areas in an unfamiliar lake, a very productive tactic year-round, but especially late spring into fall, and again in mid-winter when trout are feeding in the top 20 feet of water. It is also one of the few techniques that consistently produces large lake trout from extreme depths. You can adjust the depth at which you fish by adjusting sinker weight and boat speed. The slower your boat speed the deeper your bait trolls. Whenever I start out I experiment with both speed and depth to locate fish.

Rigs can be as the basic as a sinker, hook and bait, or as complicated as illustrated drop sinker and flasher blade rigs. Flashers help significantly to attract trout to the bait and for many trollers it's the only way to fish. The mega drawing power of flashers allows trollers to use tiny baits that are normally too insignificant to attract fish from any distance. The use of blade strings allows trollers to use tiny trout favorites like single salmon eggs, maggots, nymphs, hellgrammites, kernels of corn and tiny earth worms. Flashers do, however, add considerable weight and dampen the fight of anything but a lunker fish. When rigging flasher blades, use a minimum of 8-pound test mainline, and insert a rubber snubber (see diagram below) to soften the shock when ripping strikes hit taut lines.

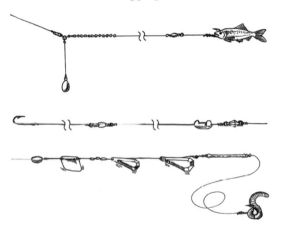

Chapter 6
To the Table: Release Your Trout to Fight Again or Turn It Into Finger-Lickin' Tablefare

Tomorrow's fishing depends on today's enthusiastic support of catch-and-release fishing. I strongly advocate releasing trout—dinks and whoppers—and all wild trout, and take great care not to injure fish. Wet both hands if you have to handle the trout, unhook it in the water, keep fingers out of the gills, don't squeeze, and never rip the hook free.

Science proves that in most cases catch-and-release fishing contributes to longer fishing seasons (reversing the old put-and-take mentality that saw many lakes "fished out" by May), keeps more large trout in the fishery, and increases the survival of natural spawners—all of which really fires up fishing fever enthusiasm. Nothing hooks a new fisherman like catching fish.

However, catch-and-release is not always possible or even desirable. Fish and game departments raise thousands of hatchery trout that are released specifically to be caught and eaten. When the fish population is allowed to surge unchecked and overrun the food supply, small lakes may become crammed with stunted trout. Overcrowding is especially common in still waters with fast-reproducing brook trout. A skillet sizzling with pan-size brookies is almost always a good thing.

One of the unfortunate but realistic facts about bait-fishing is that trout bite to eat. Bait is often swallowed and hooks sink into delicate gills, throat or vital organs. More often than not, these wounds will eventually kill the fish—either from the severity of the wound or from later infections.

Wounded trout die, whether they are released or kept. The only difference is who eats them—bullheads, bugs and beetles, or you.

Fish hooked anywhere other than the lips, that are bleeding, accidentally dropped and bounced around the bottom of the boat, or squeezed with a bit too much enthusiasm should be kept, cleaned, eaten, and smiled about.

The first step toward the skillet is to bleed the trout. When trout are not bled immediately after being caught, blood pools in the meat and it develops that "fishy" taste and smell some diners find disagreeable. Use a knife or your finger to cut (or tear) the gills.

Cleaning

1. Insert a fillet knife (or scissors) into the anal cavity and cut through the belly to the base of the gill rakers.

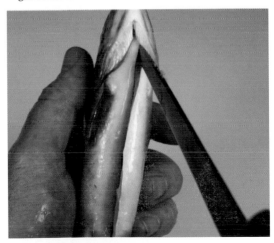

2. Cut through the lower throat (and over the tongue) as pictured.

3. Where you made the cut in Step 2, insert your thumb into the lower jaw to hold the fish in place. Firmly grasp the tongue and base of the gill rakers (with your other hand) and pull out the tongue, gill rakers and innards of the fish.

4. Scrape the swim bladder (sometimes called the
   bloodline) from the backbone with your thumb,
   a small spoon or old toothbrush.

Filleting

1. Make an incision through the flesh, but short of
   the organs, from behind the head, behind the
   pectoral fin to the stomach. Do not sever backbone. Both sides.

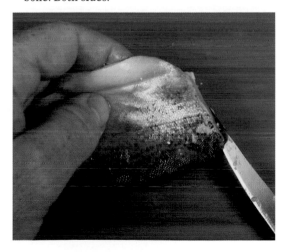

2. Cut along the back with the flat of the knife pressed against and riding along the spine, and the point ticking the top of the rib cage. Once behind the ribs, push the blade through the body and out the bottom of the fish near the vent. Continue cutting to tail. Both sides.

3. Carefully carve meat down and over the rib cage. Both sides.

4. Place the fillet on a board, scale side down. Pin the tail end of the fillet to the board with your fingers, insert the knife blade just above fingertips, slice down to the skin, and with the blade slightly angled down and away, slide the blade smoothly to the front, separating the meat from the skin.

5. Soak fillet in salted water to eliminate remnants of blood for an hour or two before freezing or frying.
6. Freeze fillets in water-filled containers (milk cartons, plastic bags) to retain fresh flavor.

Ethics & Manners: Keys to Fishing Fun

- Limit and eat your kill.

- Practice and teach catch-and-release.

- Respect the life of your catch—big or small, it gave its all.

- Treat the fishermen on the far side of the water like they were on yours.

- Never crowd others, especially when they're catching fish.

- Ask, don't intrude.

- Keep your shadow off the fishing water.

- Listen to the wild, not the radio; nothing is as annoying as someone else's music.

- Pets always belong on leashes.

- After a reasonable time enjoying the "hot spot," move and invite others to share.

- Don't cross lines.

- Don't boat fish in a bank fisherman's water, or cast from the bank into a boater's area.

- Quietly untangle crossed lines, yelling won't help.

- Rat's nest tangles: Cut your line, free theirs, re-rig.

- Stow extra gear at your feet.

- Yield water to anyone playing a fish.

- Do not impose yourself on others.

- Wait, don't cut in front.

- Offer left-over bait to others.

- Don't harass fish on spawning redds.

- When entering an occupied stream drift, follow the other angler or wait until he or she's fished it through.

- Rig boats, test motors before launching.

- Don't block boat launches with boats, trailers, lawn chairs, tackle boxes or forked sticks.

- Boats have right-of-way at boat docks.

- See litter? Pick it up, pack it out.

- Pocket discarded fishing line.

- When someone asks for help, give it.

- Warming fires: Burn it all, put it out, scatter the rocks and leave no trace.

- Practice the Golden Rule: Ask yourself, would I find it offensive if somebody did this to me?

- Hand off hookups to beginners.

- Leave your rod at home and teach someone to enjoy fishing.

- Beverage cans: If you packed it in full, you can pack it out empty.